REEL ISSU
Engaging film and faith

IAN MAHER

GW01393015

Contents

The **open** *Book*

BIBLE SOCIETY

1 Did you see . . . ?

As we near the dawn of a new millennium a hugely significant "common currency" is already shared by large numbers of people, and it isn't called the Euro. Unlike the awaited financial currency, this currency is a cultural one and one that is riding a new wave of popularity. Consisting of briefly experienced images and sound, film is a currency with the power to touch emotions and reshape the way we see the world. Widely used by some of the groups who have least contact with the Church, film is a communication medium that churches ignore at their peril. As a vehicle through which major themes of life can be engaged – themes also addressed in the Bible – film represents an unsurpassed and exciting opportunity for churches to reach out to people for whom the Bible is currently a closed book.

People engage with films to such an extent that conversations in the pub or coffee bar often include a "did you see . . . ?" question. And next time you are leaving the cinema just listen out to the conversations taking place as people leave the auditorium.

In an age of visual media, films have a power and immediacy that connect with people in a way that stereotypical views of Bible study sometimes lack. It is as though people need a new means of connecting with the timeless Story of God's love for His people. As we will see, this "common currency" of film has enormous potential for making this connection. But first, let us consider a few statistics.

So who is watching?

In 1997, cinema attendance alone in the UK was 137 million[1], an increase of 58.5 million from ten years earlier when the total was 78.5 million[2]. An average of over 2.6 million people are therefore attending the cinema each week. This boom in popularity is also reflected in the increase of cinema screens in the UK, many of which are part of the new multiplex centres. In 1986 there were 660 sites with a total of 1,249 screens. By 1996 the figure was 742 sites and 2,166 screens[3].

The breakdown of exactly who is going to the cinema in terms of age group also makes fascinating reading: 80% of the UK's 7- to 14-year-olds and 83% of 15- to 24-year-olds visit the cinema at least two or three times per year. The figures for the 25 to 34 and 35+ age groups are 64% and 27% respectively[4]. The young people so conspicuous by their absence in many of our churches are frequenting the cinema in their millions in the course of a year.

Of course, cinema-going is just the tip of the iceberg. A total 79 million videos were sold during 1996 and 230 million videos were rented by a population of 51.75 million people[5]. In other words, an average of at least one video was purchased and four videos rented by every person in the UK.

In 1996 the top 20 feature films alone broadcast on terrestrial television attracted a total of 209.26 million viewers[6]. The same year saw totals of 2.24 million and 3.79 million cable and satellite subscribers respectively, representing further avenues for film watching[7].

While statistics can be bewildering, one thing comes through with absolute clarity: people are watching films in numbers surpassing regular church attendance, and significantly so in respect of people between the ages of 7 and 35. What if it were possible to find a way to help film-watchers make some practical links between the stories which entertain and move them and the Story of the Bible? What if films could become a means of "opening the Book"?

Making sense of things

In the recent publication *Explorations in Theology and Film*, David Browne comments: "Film shows us ourselves, and is a mirror both of our achievements and of our strivings; we make meaning in all that we do, whether this is done to illuminate our path or to search for the infinite. In learning to read a film, we become fluent in interpreting the language of life."[8].

What better reason could there be for searching out ways of connecting our understanding of God, as portrayed through the cultural expressions of the Bible, with insights into God carried by perhaps the most powerful medium of late 20th century culture? The power of film should not be underestimated. It connects with the deepest of human emotions and feelings. Tears at the cinema may very well be a result of connecting with something very personal.

Used wisely, films can be a very positive means of engaging with issues that really matter. A caution is needed, however, since films can also be used manipulatively. This should be avoided at all costs. In addition, for reasons outlined above, films engage with life's big questions. One of the reasons why people watch films is that what they see on screen rings bells with their own experiences, struggles and questions. Sometimes this happens in obvious ways; sometimes it is more subtle. Often the answers suggested by films are simplistic and inadequate, but the fact that the questions are raised provides a point of contact that the Church really cannot afford to ignore if it takes contemporary society seriously.

In the pages that follow are some insights into what it is about film that has the capacity to engage with such large numbers of people in sometimes deep and important ways. Then comes a section which looks at some principles for using film to engage with biblical themes, followed by some guidelines and practical suggestions. Finally, in the section *Now Showing*, there are two worked examples of using film for each of the five themes identified by the Open Book project as central biblical and human interests: Identity, Freedom, Justice, Hope and Forgiveness. It is hoped that these pages will play their part in throwing open both these interests and the Bible to friends and film-watchers inside and outside of the Church.

2 *The power of film*

There are numerous reasons why films are such a powerful medium, whether viewed at the cinema, or on video or television. They engage with us through at least two different levels.

The conscious level

Films engage our intellect and our emotions. There will be much taking place within a film that we are aware of, or could become more aware of. For example, the plot of the film to which we can bring a critical approach. We may agree or want to contend strongly against the message of the film. Soundtrack and scenery are also ways in which we become affected by film (especially on the big screen). Musical and visual impact can effectively bypass our thought processes and plug in directly to us at an emotional level. It is one reason why films make us cry. Although we know that the characters on screen are professional actors playing out a script, nevertheless, the tears still flow. This is hardly surprising when we stop to realise that being human is not simply about thinking. We are also emotional and feeling beings. Film can touch every aspect of our being.

The unconscious level

The discipline of psychology tells us that much of our existence is affected by our unconscious drives and motives. Our various life experiences have a deep and lasting effect upon us, even though much of this might lie below the surface of our conscious awareness. Very often we are aware of why a film's subject matter or treatment challenges or disturbs us. But at other times films may connect with our unconscious and trigger responses which initially seem puzzling, perhaps out of all proportion to the film's content. It can be very disconcerting when waves of grief are brought on by a fairly innocuous section of film, but I have seen it happen a number of times. However, when we reflect upon such a reaction, we may realise that the film is connecting very strongly with something from a past event or something current in our own lives.

Sometimes, despite all attempts to get to the root of the response, the real reason remains hidden in our unconscious. It is important that we reassure ourselves, or someone that we know who is affected in this way, that such a reaction to a film is not "silly" even though there might not be a readily available explanation.

Another link between films and our unconscious is the way in which a film that we have seen years ago can resurface and connect with something in the present. Like all our experiences, watching a film has an effect and therefore has the potential to affect us at a later date.

Diverse effects

The same film can trigger very different responses in people. One person might be reduced to tears; another left unmoved. One person might be challenged, whereas another might be deeply offended. Each person brings to a film unique life experiences, values and insights and will therefore interact with the film in a unique way.

Common threads

There are, however, some common threads. A film can have the power to touch some of the same nerves in a vast number of people. For example, the screen adaptation of Michael Ondaatje's novel *The English Patient* (directed by Anthony Minghella, 1996) guaranteed hardly a dry eye in the house; the film adaptation of Thomas Keneally's *Schindler's List* (directed by Steven Spielberg, 1993) left people numb and horrified in a glimpse of the holocaust; and *Brassed Off* (directed by Mark Herman, 1996) evoked a very real sense of identification with a group of unemployed men battling against the destruction of their livelihoods at the coal pit. Three very different films, yet each touched something of a common nerve and connected audiences with very powerful themes: love and loss, life and death, the struggle of the human spirit against the odds.

Why connections happen

Aside from the vast marketing enterprise that surrounds the big blockbusters, films become popular when they tap into things that really matter to a large cross-section of people. Sometimes film directors set out to connect in this way. At other times, films quite unexpectedly find success at the box office when a subject very close to a director's heart turns out to be a subject close to the hearts of many.

Four Weddings and a Funeral (directed by Mike Newell, 1994) is a prime example. Very few people anticipated its phenomenal success, yet it was a major box-office earner. Perhaps the most significant reason for this is that the film resonated with the almost universal human experience of recognising how easily life can slip by with issues of love, friendships and relationships remaining unresolved. Similarly, *The Full Monty* (directed by Peter Cattaneo, 1997) has connected with other shared experiences: what it means to be out of work and on the dole with little or no hope of a job. Yes, it is a very funny film but it also has its hard edge. Think of the character who tries to commit suicide, having lost hope of finding work again. Or the sheer, grinding monotony confronting the character who works every hour God made as a store detective in order to make ends meet. Films have the power, even through the guise of comedy, to touch us in painful spots.

The need for a critical eye

When watching films it is easy to suspend judgement about right and wrong. The viewer should always remain aware of the possibility of a subversive message "slipping under the guard"[9]. Because of the reasons outlined concerning the power of film it is important that we do not uncritically allow the sort of responses we make to characters and situations in a film to spill over into real life. A recent example of "gung-ho-ism" is *Independence Day* (directed by Roland Emmerich, 1996). There is a clear distinction between the "goodies" (humankind – especially the Americans) and the "baddies" (aliens intent on conquering earth). Packed full of action, the film portrays how the Americans, through their military might and especially through their ingenuity, save the day. Confined within the realms of entertainment the film is a lot of fun. The problem arises when the sentiments of such films spill over into real-life conflicts where issues of morality are seldom clear-cut, and right and wrong are grey areas rather than certainties. We need to be aware that films can, if watched uncritically, manipulate us into making judgements based on the particular viewpoint of the director. Life is more complex and the sort of "knee-jerk" responses that films sometimes evoke are seldom appropriate.

Portraying or shaping us?

As a major cultural expression, films have the power both to reflect and shape our society. They invariably portray ways of seeing and understanding something of the world in which we live. Such worldviews can support, challenge or subvert the political, moral, philosophical and religious foundations on which our society is built. For example, the 1992 film *Falling Down*, starring Michael Douglas (directed by Joel Schumacher) takes a wry look at the pressures of urban life in modern-day America, suggesting that the American dream is far from a reality.

Irrespective of whether obvious religious themes are present, films say something about the world in which we live and about the values we live by. Their sheer pervasiveness affords a huge potential for influence. This should not be underestimated. Just as politics is too important for the Church to leave to politicians, film is far too influential for us not to engage with as Christians. Without such engagement there is no way of knowing how we as a society are portrayed by, and how much we are shaped by, the films that are made and viewed by millions. Equally, not to engage with film would be to miss opportunities to offer biblical responses to the central human concerns that films are conveying.

3 *Engaging with biblical themes*

Films, as we have seen, can make contact in people with the things that matter in life. We should not be surprised at this if we believe in a God who is active and present in the world. God has always worked through cultural expression to make himself known. This is an important reason why there can be some very natural connections between issues raised by films and those explored within the pages of the Bible. In each case the human condition is being addressed, portrayed and interpreted.

Common questions

Some of the most common questions are Who am I? What am I here for? Where am I going? Why is there suffering? They are just some of the questions that recur time and time again in films. Sometimes they are answered in a very simplistic way which ignores the complexity of life. But, nevertheless, the questions are very often there in a film if you scratch beneath the surface, even if they are not immediately obvious.

Different frameworks but recurring issues

Christians, agnostics, atheists and followers of other perspectives have different worldviews to bring to bear upon a film, but the issues themselves are common ones. In seeking answers to life's big questions, people may start from different reference points and use a different vocabulary, but the questions are essentially the same. Time and again the same issues crop up in films. This is because of, and sometimes in spite of, the director. "Being human" questions inevitably surface with great regularity and sometimes new films are simply a variation on a well used theme.

Engaging faith and film

Dialogue is the key. Faith issues need to be brought alongside the film and the two be allowed to interact. God is active in the world today so we ought to have an openness to our faith being informed and changed by film. If we are serious about this task, we need to be open to the possibility that film will challenge us and sometimes cause us to rethink our understanding and expression of the faith we hold dear.

Sacred and secular films

This is an unhelpful and, in fact, false distinction. If there is a difference, it rests in the fact that the same issues are looked at through different lenses. The human condition is the same. To make a rigid sacred/secular distinction is effectively limiting God and suggesting that he can only speak through overtly religious films. This is like saying that we can only experience God in church on Sundays. Religious films can, of course, be powerful means of engaging people in discussion and exploration of faith matters in an appropriate setting. For many "unchurched" people, "secular" films are often a better starting point.

A vital encounter

Films frequently raise important issues and pressing concerns. It is a medium which has an immediate impact and power and has huge potential to influence people for good or bad. Alternative viewpoints and philosophies of life are also communicated to huge audiences. Consequently, film presents Christians with a unique opportunity to meet film-watchers on their own turf and enter into dialogue which might never have otherwise been possible.

4 *Using film: some practical tips*

This section is designed to help you use films as a means of generating questions, discussion and deeper exploration of faith and related issues. It will be of particular use to those involved in leadership within the local church who want to take the phenomenon of film seriously and make the most of the "common currency" that it represents.

Teachers can look at similar points with sixth formers in schools. Here experience suggests that you will find a more receptive audience if you first look at one or two films which clearly express non-religious worldviews. In this way, students will grasp that religious people are not alone in having a view of the world and the idea of discussing Christian themes will become less difficult.

Strategies for film watching

Depending upon the situation, your use of film will vary in terms of the depth in which you tackle the subject and the angle from which you approach it. You may, for example, be reviewing a film for a Christian magazine or such like. You may be reviewing for a secular publication. It is important in such contexts that you pay due attention to assessing the film from a film point of view as well as from a faith point of view.

However, it is likely that in the context of Christian ministry, your main use of film will relate to connecting people with major themes. Life's big issues in other words, and what the Christian faith has to say about them. For such use you are looking for a number of things which are applicable irrespective of whether or not the film in question is technically (that is, from a film-maker's point of view) a good one. Here are some points to use as a framework for watching a film with a view to then using it with a group of people, whether for theological exploration, pastoral or evangelistic reasons.

An overview

It is important to have an overview of the film. In other words, you need to be able to summarise concisely to yourself what the film is about. Three key questions are: What is the film about? What are its main themes? Who are the main characters? To gain a reasonable overview will involve watching the film at least once before using it in a group setting.

The Director's intention

As far as you can tell, is the director trying to make a particular point? What do you regard as the message the director is trying to convey? In your use of the film you might want to challenge these intentions. For example, if a film conveys a very pessimistic view of the future, it might be useful to bring into conversation with the film the alternative of Christian hope.

Life's big questions

Allied to the theme(s) of the film are often some of life's big questions. Some thoughts to bear in mind are: What does the film say about human nature? Does it promote a particular view of the world? What does it say about human relationships? The film might conflict sharply with the Christian position on such matters, but again this offers the possibility to open up dialogue.

The faith connection

Moving on a step, the next series of questions to bear in mind are: What specific characters and scenes ring bells with theological themes and/or issues of faith? Is the Christian perspective on life challenged, undermined or supported by the film's message?

Some other points to consider . . .

If it is a film of a book or a play with which you are familiar, do you think the director's intention is different to the writer's? Who do you think the viewer is meant to identify with? (This could be one or several characters from the film).

And so to the next step . . .

When you have reached this level of familiarity with the film, you are ready to consider ways of using these insights to develop group sessions in which people can engage with the film.

5 *The use of film in groups*

Once you have made a decision about which film(s) to use, the next task is to decide how you will proceed. By the time you reach this point you should have a good knowledge about the film(s) in question. For the purpose of engaging faith and film it is not vital to know such things as actors' names or who is behind the camera. There are, however, details that you should know in order to facilitate the group effectively. Here is a checklist that will help you in your task.

The film rating

Sensitivity is required to ensure that films are not shown to those who are under the designated age-rating. It is, however, almost inevitable that many under-18s, for example, will have seen "18" category films and there is no reason why they should be discouraged from any discussion groups and helped to wrestle with issues raised. Care does need to be taken, however, not to encourage people in breaking the rating restrictions.

Know the storyline

You need to be able to give a brief overview of what the story is about. It is not always necessary to share this with the group but it needs to be at your fingertips and is helpful particularly when your group only has the opportunity to see sections of a film and when people have not seen the film in its entirety.

Know the main characters

In some films the number of actors make it difficult to remember all the names. You should, however, be familiar with the main characters.

Be aware of the faith themes that you believe relate to the film

Sometimes these will be obvious; sometimes they will need teasing out. It is important that you can, if necessary, draw out some of the themes that might be implicit in a film. In a group setting this is like opening the box.

Be aware of which biblical stories (if any) the film relates to

Not all films ring bells with biblical stories, but some do. Be aware of such parallels that do emerge in order that you might feed them into the group.

Decide how you will show the film

You will need to plan how people see the film. It is always best if people have had the opportunity of watching the entire film before working together as a group. A practical way of doing this is to organise a social gathering one week at which people watch the video. The following week, come together and reconnect with the film by showing specific clips that you feel are appropriate. A similar exercise can be carried out with a film on release at the cinema and not yet out on video, with the limitation that the group session would need to rely on memory of the film without the aid of film clips. It is possible to explore a film in a single session or develop its use over a series of evenings. Even weekends based around a film are possible.

Planning the session

When you are familiar enough with the film you intend to use, the next thing to tackle is how to use the time with a group. There are many ways of using the film to help people engage with the issues raised. The following are some possibilities but the options are limited only by your imagination.

Brainstorm

Gather in immediate responses from the group about emotions and feelings stirred up by the film or to a particular question that you might like to pose. These could be written up on a flipchart or large piece of paper and opportunity provided for people to elaborate on their initial comments, moving into discussion where appropriate.

Use pairs and small group exercises

This gives people the opportunity to wrestle with issues raised by the film in a more intimate way than in the large group. Exercises can include responses to tasks that you introduce relating to the film and/or group members' own experiences.

Feedback session and whole group discussions

Sometimes it is appropriate for small groups to feed back the findings of their deliberations into a whole group discussion, particularly when groups have tackled different but related tasks.

Role-play

This will depend on the nature of the group but, if sensitively handled, is possible in many groups. Ask individuals in the group to assume the role of a character from the film. Then encourage a conversation to take place between the characters (you may need to prompt the conversation with some opening questions or comments). A variation on this is for the role-playing people to enter into conversation with the non role-players.

Creative responses

In some cases, a helpful approach is to provide people with the means of responding non-verbally to the film. For example, through drawing, painting, collage, or sculpture with clay.

Some general questions

1. **Ask the group what issues the film raised for them.** You will have your own ideas of the main issues, but it is important that the group discover these together. Often the group will identify issues that you have overlooked.

2. **Ask the group if the film rings any bells with biblical stories/issues of faith.** This is a way of opening up discussion, but be sensitive to the group you are working with and avoid religious jargon.

3. **Ask people which character(s) in the film they most identify with and why.** This can sometimes be a helpful way for people to express something of their own journey through life from a "safe distance". Some people find that relating to a character in a film helps them to face the issues and struggles in their own lives.

4. **Ask people to consider the film in relation to Christian faith.** For instance, does the film challenge or support Christian values? Are there Christ-like figures in the film and, if so, in what way? If the film raises hard questions, what are the Christian responses to those questions?

An evangelistic postscript

Each of the above points are relevant to using film in an evangelistic setting, but in addition a few extra points are worth noting.

Recognise the "good news" themes present

As with the use of films for general faith exploration, in using film for evangelistic purposes you should seek to identify some ways in which the gospel message connects with some of the film's big issues. What is the good news for the situation portrayed? Why and how does Christianity make a difference? How does faith in Jesus Christ inform, support or challenge situations and relationships within the film?

Are people likely to have seen the film?

If you are using a film for evangelistic purposes, there are likely to be people present who are not part of your regular church fellowship. They might not have had the same opportunity as others in the group to view the film before, perhaps at a previous housegroup. It is therefore important to ensure that any film used is a popular film that people are likely to have seen or one for which they at least have a knowledge of the storyline. In some cases it will be appropriate to find ways for people to see the film in advance of any discussion. A separate occasion for viewing the film is desirable. Using a film, or films, in the context of an evangelistic course rather than a single event is usually preferable to a one-off event for the reasons mentioned above.

What films are people currently watching?

Keep an eye out in the media to discover which are the popular films. The "blockbusters" may not always be the best films from a technical or aesthetic point of view, but these films above others are "common currency" within our society. Look closely at the main points the films examine and consider ways of explaining how Christian faith can bring a different perspective to bear. All the while, keep in mind the question: "What is good news in relation to this film?"

Relevance to the group

This may be stating the obvious, but care is needed to ensure that no offence is caused to a group by the wrong choice of film. Clearly, very little evangelistic opportunity will ensue if people walk out! It goes without saying that you will need to consider carefully the interests of the group with which you are working. The whole experience needs to be relevant and interesting.

Do not limit yourself to overtly religious films

"Secular" films pick up all the major themes of faith, sometimes in subtle rather than overt ways. Christians should not be discouraged from using popular films that are not specifically "Christian". There is usually plenty of material to unearth, whatever the film might be. The fact that a film is not overtly religious often makes it far less threatening to an interested enquirer.

Encourage people to face up to the questions

Encourage people and gently enable them to identify with the questions and issues posed by the film. The Christian position might agree with or challenge the film and here lies the opportunity to share the good news of Jesus Christ in an appropriate way. Do not feel that you have to "give the gospel" every time you open your mouth. Instead, be sensitive to whatever the film is raising within members of the group and opportunities will come.

Be honest about what you are doing

It is always wrong to bring people together under false pretences. If you intend to use a film for evangelistic purposes, be open about it. Let people know that you will be seeking to bring a gospel perspective to bear upon the film. That way, you avoid the danger of making people feel that they have been manipulated. It is a bad witness to try and bring evangelism in through the back door.

NOW SHOWING

Some worked examples

The following ten worked examples pick up the Open Book themes of Identity, Freedom, Justice, Hope and Forgiveness. In these cases the approach has been to start with a theme and then engage with a suitable film rather than begin with the film and look for the themes that emerge. This has enabled a direct connection to be made with the Open Book project. Each example would take approximately one-and-a-half hours to work through with a group, though this will depend on the amount of time allowed for the various exercises.

STAR TREK : FIRST CONTACT

PARAMOUNT

F I L M

Directed
by
Jonathan
Frakes

CERT **12**

1996

The film story

In a plot that twists and turns, Captain Jean-Luc Picard (Patrick Stewart) and his crew of the Starship Enterprise E engage in a battle with the Borg which takes them from the 24th century to the 21st. The Borg, a race of half-biological, half-mechanical life-forms, travel back in time in an attempt to destroy earth's first warp-speed flight. In doing so, they would prevent first contact with a race of passing aliens and the subsequent formation of the Federation of Planets. The storyline switches between earth, and events aboard the Enterprise E. On earth, frantic efforts are made to help Zefram Cochrane (James Cromwell) repair his Borg-damaged spaceship before its maiden voyage. On the Enterprise, Picard and his crew battle to prevent the ship from being assimilated as a result of Borg infiltration. Eventually, the Borg are defeated, Cochrane's vessel makes a successful flight and first contact is established. In a fascinating sub-plot involving the android, Lieutenant Commander Data (Brent Spiner), Data longs to know what it is to be human. When captured by the Borg Queen (Alice Krige), he discovers that the human condition encompasses both pain and pleasure. It is within the frailty of flesh and blood that human relationships and identity are formed.

Some key issues
The importance of individuality – this is highlighted by the extreme contrast of the Borg collective, where each "individual" exists only to service the collective and every individual is expendable for the good of the race.

What it means to be human – Data discovers first hand the pain and temptation that are part of the human nature for which, as an android, he yearns.

Identity defined in relation to others – Data's loyalty and commitment to his crew enable him to overcome the temptation offered by the Borg Queen for his own self-fulfilment. Also, Picard puts his own life on the line to save Data, his friend.

Clips

Show the section of film where the Borg Queen argues her case with Data that the striving of the Borg towards perfection takes precedence over the life of any particular race.

Group discussion:
From your knowledge of the 20th century, does this ring any bells for you?

Show the sections where Data experiences both pain and pleasure while captive to the Borg Queen.

Group discussion:
What insights into being human do you think that Data's encounter with the Borg Queen provided him with? Could Data ever understand pain and pleasure without experiencing them?

Show the section where the Enterprise E is being evacuated and Picard makes the decision to remain on board to try and rescue Data.

Group discussion:
Why did Picard put his life on the line for Data?

Our story

In pairs:
Share with each other any personal experiences that you have had of not being valued as a unique human being. How did they make you feel? What sort of long-term effect do you think such treatment would have on a person?

Feedback and discussion:
Gather in some points from the exercise in pairs and list them on a large sheet of paper. See if any common threads emerge. Allow opportunity for people to discuss what they regard as the underlying reasons for the undermining of a person's self-worth.

Individual exercise:
Draw on a sheet of paper a line representing your life. Mark on the line, in words or pictures, some significant moments of pain or joy.

Group discussion:
Share with each other ways in which events, good or bad, from your life line have shaped your own identity. How different are you as a person because of them?

Small groups (3 or 4 people):
What is it that makes a human being willing to sacrifice his or her life for someone else? What do you think this says about human identity? Think of some times when other people have put themselves out for you. How did you feel? Think of some times when you have put yourself out for others. What were your reasons?

God's story

Identity is a vital component of being human. It is that sense of who we are in relation to each other and to God which defines us and gives us our sense of self-worth. Loss of identity can easily result in a sense of sense of despair, as we end up feeling like nothing more than cogs in a machine. The Bible, however, provides us with constant reminders that each and every one of us matters to God and is loved and valued by him in a unique way. For example, Psalm 139 reminds us of God's complete knowledge and care for us: "Lord, you have examined me and you know me. You know everything I do; from far away you understand all my thoughts" (Psalm 139.1, 2). In the New Testament, Jesus offers a wonderful reminder of God's amazing love for us: "For only a penny you can buy two sparrows, yet not one sparrow falls to the ground without your Father's consent. As for you, even the hairs of your head have all been counted. So do not be afraid; you are worth much more than many sparrows!" (Matthew 10.29–31). St Paul reminds us: "Those who are led by God's Spirit are God's children. For the Spirit that God has given you does not make you slaves and cause you to be afraid; instead, the Spirit makes you God's children, and by the Spirit's power we cry out to God, 'Father! My Father!' God's Spirit joins himself to our spirits to declare that we are God's children" (Romans 8.14–17). If we take the Bible seriously, it will profoundly deepen and enrich our sense of intrinsic worth as unique individuals created in the image and likeness of God.

Group exercise:
From the film considered, recall as many instances as you can where individuals seemed to count for very little. What reasons can you think of for this? Repeat the exercise, but this time recall instances where individuals were appreciated and valued.

Role play or group discussion:
If several people are willing, ask them to imagine that they are characters from the film considered (for example, Borg soldiers from *Star Trek: First Contact* or miners facing redundancy in *Brassed Off*). Ask them, in character, to say something of how it feels to be treated like tiny cogs in a large machine. Do they feel worthless and why? If the role-play is too threatening, simply ask people to talk about how they think the characters in the film must have felt.

Group exercise:
Read Psalm 139.1–18. The psalmist points us towards a God who loves and values us not for what we do but for who we are, in relation to God and to each other. This can be a great comfort in a world that does the opposite. Share with each other any ways in which this truth has helped you in your pilgrimage through life. Draw the session to a close by asking each person in turn to say to the group: "I am (name). There has never been and will never be another me. I am a child of God and he loves me with an everlasting love."

Close with a short time of reflection and prayer.

CHANNEL 4 / MIRAMAX

F I L M

BRASSED OFF

Directed by Mark Herman

CERT 15

1996

The film story

The members of the Grimley Colliery Band are living in uncertain times as their Yorkshire pit faces closure. Their lives are brightened somewhat by the arrival of Gloria (Tara Fitzgerald), the beautiful granddaughter of a former band member. Unknown to the men, Gloria is working for the Coal Board but genuinely believes that her feasibility study will ensure the survival of the pit. An accomplished musician, she is allowed to join the colliery band.

Brassed Off follows the lives of various members of the band and shows how a number of them have lost their sense of self-worth. For example, Phil (Stephen Tompkinson) attempts suicide following pressure from loan sharks collecting on old debts incurred during the 1984 miners' strike. Then there is Harry (Jim Carter) who is seen several times arriving home as his wife leaves for work, with no more than a few curt exchanges passing between them. The Grimley miners, who ten years earlier had stood tall and assured, become resigned to the inevitable closure of their pit.

For a time the colliery band seems to be the only thing that gives the Grimley men a sense of identity. Band leader Danny (Pete Postlethwaite) has steered them through to the national brass band finals at the Royal Albert Hall. However, even the band falls apart when the closure of the pit is announced. For example, Gloria's link with the Coal Board is discovered and she is ostracised by the men. Meanwhile, Danny has been rushed to hospital suffering the effects of pneumoconiosis.

The film draws to a conclusion when Gloria, having seen through her employer's deception, offers to put up the money to fund the band's trip to the finals. The band wins the finals and Danny, having left his sick bed to be at the Albert Hall, delivers not a victory speech but a scathing attack on a government and system that treats human beings as statistics.

Some key issues
The value of people – human beings are more than units of production.

Self-worth – how easily this can be undermined.

Undermining identity – the impact upon people of being treated as statistics on a balance sheet.

Identity defined in relation to others – the colliery band gives the miners a sense of purpose and belonging.

Clips

Show the section of the film where Phil returns home to find his wife and children leaving, following the visit of the loan sharks who have taken possession of all of the family furniture.

Group discussion:
What do you think must have been going on in Phil's mind at that point, as his family disappeared into the distance, his children waving forlornly through the van window? What do you think this experience did to Phil's sense of self-esteem? Write up the main points of your discussion on a large sheet of paper.

Show the section where the Grimley Colliery Band play what they think will be their last concert for band leader Danny as he lies very ill in hospital.

Group discussion:
What do you think was going through Danny's mind when the band struck up? What do you think this experience did to Danny's sense of self-esteem? Write up the main points of your discussion on a large sheet of paper.

Group activity:
Compare the two lists and share any thoughts on the things that tear down and the things that build up a person's sense of identity and self-esteem.

Show the section of the film where Danny gives his "acceptance" speech following the band's victory at the Royal Albert Hall.

Brainstorm:
Gather in immediate responses to Danny's speech. Write up thoughts and feelings expressed on a large sheet of paper.

Our story

Group discussion:
Talk together about any ways in which the film rings bells with your own experience. For example, someone in the group might have experienced redundancy.

Small group activity:
Think for a moment about the person in *Brassed Off* that you most identify with. Share with each other the reasons for your choice.

Group activity and discussion:
List on a large sheet of paper any times in your own life when your sense of identity and self-worth has been undermined by the behaviour and attitudes of others. Talk about any common factors that emerge in this activity.

God's story (same as for *Star Trek: First Contact*)

Close with a short time of reflection and prayer.

COLUMBIA TRISTAR

FILM

AWAKENINGS

Directed
by
Penny
Marshall

CERT **15**

1990

The film story

Based on a true story, *Awakenings* tells the story of Dr Sayer (Robin Williams), a reluctant physician who arrives at a psychiatric hospital in the Bronx. There he works with a group of long-term patients who have been silent and immobile for many years with an undiagnosed illness. In a moment of insight he recognises the connection and persuades the hospital authorities to allow him to embark on a course of experimental treatment, first of all with a patient named Leonard (Robert de Niro). Over the course of a summer, first Leonard and then a whole group of patients on the treatment "awaken" and are freed from the constraints of their illness. Unfortunately, the recovery is temporary and they slowly slide back to their totally dependent existence. However, the carers have also undergone a transformation. Freed from the numbing effect of feeding and washing unresponsive patients for years on end, the events of the summer awaken in them the realisation that these are living, breathing people, vibrant and alive despite being locked within an illness which cuts them off from normal communication. The approach of the carers is dramatically changed.

Some key issues

Loss of freedom due to illness – the patients had been made totally dependent upon others for everything.

Feeling paralysed in face of suffering – Dr Sayer believed at the beginning that there was nothing that could be done for the patients.

Becoming trapped by routine – until Dr Sayers' arrival, the hospital had virtually given up on the patients.

Breaking out of a blinkered approach to life – before the summer "awakening" the carers saw their patients as collections of symptoms. When summer came, they saw people.

Clips

Show the section of the film when Dr Sayer and his staff are discovering that they can evoke responses from patients to particular sounds and actions.

Ask members of your group to consider what it might have felt like to be one of the patients in the film before Dr Sayer's intervention. What must it have been like to be trapped like that in a motionless body? Encourage people to share with each other, in a sentence or two, their responses.

Show the section beginning with Leonard's awakening up to the point where he "paddles" in the sea.

How do you think Leonard and Dr Sayer must have felt during this time?

Show the final section of the film from the point at which Leonard has reverted to his motionless state.

In what ways do you think the "awakening" summer changed the approach of the carers?

Our story

Small group discussion:

1. Think of times in your own life when your freedom has been curtailed, perhaps by illness or loss of income. Take a moment or two to describe to each other how that made you feel. What were the hardest things for you in such situations?

2. *Awakenings* showed how, before that dramatic summer, the patients not only suffered loss of freedom brought on by their illness but also from the somewhat indifferent and impersonal attitudes of their carers. Have there been times when you have been oppressed by the attitudes of others (some form of prejudice, perhaps)?

Group discussion:
Where and why do you think freedom is taken for granted? Discuss this and write up your main points on a large sheet of paper.

God's story

The Bible portrays freedom as a vital feature in the life of the people of God. The pivotal event in the Old Testament was God leading the Israelites from slavery in Egypt through the wilderness and into the Promised Land (Exodus 1—24; for a summary see Joshua 24). In the New Testament we read of Jesus Christ, through all that his life, death and resurrection accomplished, restoring us to a relationship with God. Through Jesus, if we turn to him in faith, we are freed from the consequences of the times when we let God down. In John's gospel we read that Jesus said "If you obey my teaching, you are really my disciples; you will know the truth, and the truth will set you free" (John 8.31–32). There is a freedom that comes in following Christ that enables us to live life to the full. In that freedom we recognise God as a loving parent and relate to each other as sisters and brothers, valuing all people as created in the likeness of God.

The implications of this freedom are corporate as well as individual. Jesus himself was fierce in confronting the oppressive religious and political structures of his day (e.g. Luke 11.37–54). The values of God's Kingdom, which Jesus ushered in, are also directly opposed to any organisation, institution, or structure which diminishes human freedom and dignity. The freedom Christ brings should spill over into communities, societies and nations until the day when the whole earth shares in this freedom and the Kingdom is established in all its fullness. The films in this section highlight some ways in which freedom can be lost, recovered and appreciated anew.

Whole group exercise:
Think of some instances from the film that has been considered where freedom, in whatever form, was lost or restricted, then brainstorm some of the reasons for this. List your points on a large sheet of paper.

Small group exercise:
Recall from your own life some occasions when you have felt oppressed by the actions of other people. Share this with each other.

Recall from your own life some occasions when you have felt "set free" by the actions of other people. Share this with each other.

Whole group exercise:
Read Joshua 24. One person could read aloud the whole chapter. Other alternatives would be to allocate sections of the chapter to a number of people. Notice how with freedom comes responsibility (Joshua 24.14–28).

Small group discussion:
"Christ has set us free!" (see Galatians 5.1). What are the implications of that truth for the way you treat other people? Try and give some examples.

Whole group exercise and discussion:
Come up with as complete a list as possible of every aspect of life in the society in which you live where freedom is lacking or restricted. What do you think an appropriate Christian response would be to some of those situations?

Close with a short time of reflection and prayer.

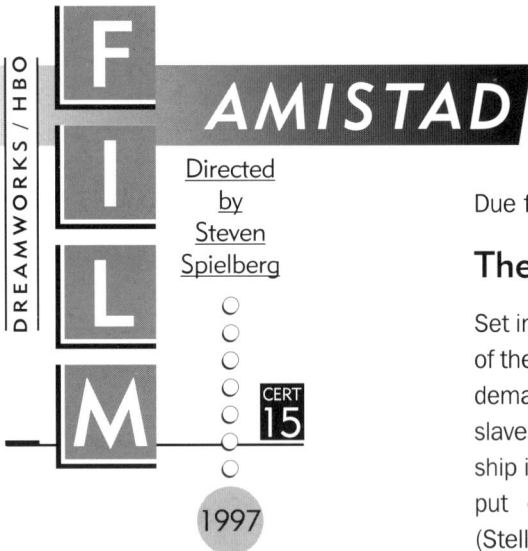

F I L M

DREAMWORKS / HBO

AMISTAD

Directed by Steven Spielberg

CERT **15**

1997

Due for release on video, Autumn, 1998

The film story

Set in 1839, *Amistad* tells the story of how 53 African slaves break free from the hold of the Spanish slave trading vessel "La Amistad". The slaves kill most of the crew and demand that the remainder take them back to Africa. From Cuba, unbeknown to the slaves, the helmsman steers along the American coastline until after weeks at sea the ship is arrested by an American naval vessel. The slaves are taken to New Haven and put on trial for murder. However, Joadson (Morgan Freeman) and Tappan (Stellan Skarsgard) – two abolitionists – take up the slaves' cause and employ Roger Baldwin (Matthew McConaughey), a young attorney, to defend them. Over time Baldwin slowly begins to understand the story being told by Cinque (Djimon Hounsou), the leader amongst the Africans. As the court case continues, the full horror of the slave trade emerges against the politics of pre-Civil War America in which concerted pressure is exerted by the pro-slavery southern states to resist the abolitionists. Eventually, following a powerful appeal to the Supreme Court from former President John Quincy Adams (Anthony Hopkins), the Africans are set free and journey home to Africa.

Some key issues
Freedom as a basic human right – the Africans in *Amistad* are treated as less than human.

The human spirit's desperate yearning to be free – the slaves seize the chance to escape, fighting to the death on the slave vessel in order to be free.

The struggle of the abolitionists to free the pro-slave lobby from their inhuman prejudices.

Clips

Show the section of the film when Cinque recounts to the court the horror of the journey on a slave trader from Africa to Cuba.

Group discussion:
Gather some immediate reactions to the clip. It is a very harrowing section of film so make sure you allow enough time for people's responses. Then discover if people feel the slaves had any other option than to kill crew members of the Amistad as they made their desperate bid for freedom. Is violence sometimes inevitable for the preservation of freedom?

Show the final section of the film where former President John Quincy Adams addresses the Supreme Court with the result that the slaves are set free.

Group discussion:
What things particularly struck you about Quincy Adams' appeal?

Our story

Small group exercise:
Look through some recent newspapers or magazines and identify stories and articles that refer to situations where human freedom is curtailed or under threat. Cut these out and paste them onto a large sheet of paper or card. *Amistad* highlighted how the vested interests of pre-Civil War American politics perpetuated the evil of slavery. Look through the cuttings that you have collected and, using a felt-tip pen, summarise in a word or two the vested interests at work behind those examples.

Whole group discussion (together as a whole group):
In what ways might people challenge such freedom-curbing practices? Discuss this together and then consider any places within your own network of contacts and relationships where there is oppression. Can anything be done to bring about change?

God's story (same as for *Awakenings*)

Close with a short time of reflection and prayer.

WARNER BROS

FILM

A TIME TO KILL

Directed
by
Joel
Schumacher

CERT **15**

1996

The film story

Set in the town of Clanton, Mississippi, this is the story of a man who takes justice into his own hands. Carl Lee Hailey (Samuel L Jackson) is the father of a ten-year-old African-American girl, Tonya (Raeven Larrymore Kelly), who was raped and left for dead by two white racists. Tonya survives, however, and the men are arrested to stand trial for rape and attempted murder. On their way to the courtroom for their preliminary hearing, Carl shoots the rapists dead. To defend him, Carl hires a struggling young lawyer, Jake Brigance (Matthew McConaughey). A plea of temporary insanity is seen as Carl's only hope.

The film unfolds against a backdrop of racial tension fuelled by Freddie Cobb (Kiefer Sutherland) who calls in the Ku Klux Klan. In a part of the United States with a history of racial abuse, Jake finds the odds stacking up against him for the courtroom battle, not least due to the selection of an all-white jury. In addition, he is forced to send his wife and daughter away from the dangers posed by the Klan. Jake's main ally in the case is Ellen Roark (Sandra Bullock), a young, rich law student opposed to the death penalty.

Dr Rodeheaver (Anthony Heald), head of a state mental hospital and one of the prosecution's main witnesses, has his credibility undermined after Ellen breaks in to his office. There she uncovers the fact that Dr Rodeheaver had found previous defendants sane, even those later committed to his institution. Jake uses this information to good effect.

Further support for the defence is given by a policeman who lost a leg after being accidentally wounded in Carl's killing of the rapists. In spite of his injuries, he is adamant in court that Carl should go unpunished: "He's a hero. You turn him loose!" In his closing statement Jake asks the jury to close their eyes, picture the awful crime, and then imagine that the little girl was white. The jury return a verdict of not guilty, and Carl is set free.

Some key issues

Justice and vengeance – there is a fine line between the two.

Punishment to fit the crime – Carl Lee Hailey believes that the attackers of his young daughter deserve the maximum penalty sanctioned by the state judicial system but that there is no likelihood of this being invoked for a crime by white men against a black girl. So he administers his own justice.

Taking the law into your own hands – Carl Lee sees no alternative to his actions if justice is to be served.

The dependence of justice upon a reliable legal system – Jake doubts that Carl Lee will receive a fair trial in a state with a sorry history of racist miscarriages of justice.

Clips

Show from the start of the film up to and including the arrest of Carl Lee Hailey following the shooting of his daughter's rapists. Before showing the clip, ask people to stay particularly aware of their emotional responses.

Small group exercise and discussion:
What emotions did the awful crime committed against little Tonya Hailey provoke in you? List these on a large sheet of paper. Then share your thoughts about Carl Lee Hailey's actions.

Group discussion:
Knowing that even a conviction, let alone a death sentence, against attackers was unlikely in a Mississippi court, Carl Lee executed them. Was this an act of justice or vengeance?

Show the section in which the policeman wounded accidentally by Carl Lee gives his testimony in court.

Group discussion:
Do you agree or disagree with the policeman's statement: "He's a hero. You turn him loose!" and for what reasons? What dangers can you see arising when justice is removed from a framework of law?

Our story

In pairs:
Discuss any incidents the media has brought to your attention to which you have responded with words such as "(s)he should be strung up for what (s)he has done". (This might be in relation to a specific offence or to a category of crime.) Why do you believe such strong emotions are evoked?

Small group discussion:
Do you think there is any instance in which you might be tempted to take the law into your own hands? For justice to be served, should the punishment always fit the crime?

Group discussion:
Talk about any experiences that you have of being on the receiving end of injustice. This might have been a major issue or a relatively small incident. How did it make you feel and what, if anything, were you able to do in addressing the injustice? List any common threads on a large sheet of paper.

God's story

God has given to us free will, making it possible to accept or reject his love. A relationship with God is not something imposed on us but a wonderful gift to which we can say "yes" or "no". There are, however, considerable responsibilities and obligations for those who respond to God's love. God looks for justice (e.g. Leviticus 19.15–16; Deuteronomy 16.18–20; Amos 8.5) tempered with mercy. The prophet Micah expresses it in this way: ". . . the Lord has told us what is good. What he requires of us is this: to do what is just, to show constant love, and to live in humble fellowship with our God" (Micah 6.8).

A measure of true justice is at one level to be found in how we exercise our responsibilities towards the marginalised and the powerless. The people of God are called to be a voice against the oppression of human dignity, with a willingness to stand against all that is dehumanising. Jesus himself offers a stark reminder of the need to take up the cause of the poor of the earth and to challenge the roots of their suffering: "I was hungry but you would not feed me, thirsty but you would not give me a drink; I was a stranger but you would not welcome me in your homes, naked but you would not clothe me; I was sick and in prison but you would not take care of me . . . I tell you, whenever you refused to help one of these least important ones, you refused to help me" (Matthew 25.42–45). At another level, justice in human society means that there must be consequences for acts which break the laws which enable people to live together. But true justice is tempered with mercy and it is this vital ingredient which avoids the danger of seeking only vengeance for wrongs committed.

Group activity and discussion:
Read Matthew 25.31–46 and consider who you regard as the hungry, the thirsty, the stranger, the prisoner, and so on, in our own society. What injustices have contributed to the plight of such people and could more be done to help them?

Group discussion:

To challenge the oppressive roots of injustice is very often a costly task. This is clear when considering, for example, the root causes of the suffering portrayed in the film. Consider times in your own life, or perhaps in the life of a friend, where making a stand for what you believe is right has carried a personal cost. Share these instances with each other.

Small group activity and discussion:

Power and prejudice are rarely far away when injustice is present. List the ways in which you feel this was true in the film considered. Then discuss God's attitude towards injustice in the light of passages such as Leviticus 19.15–16; Deuteronomy 16.18–20; Amos 8.5 and others that you are aware of. Do you think that the churches reflect God's attitude as much as they should?

Group discussion:

What do you see as the difference between justice and vengeance when thinking of a response to crimes? It might help to think of some dramatic, well publicised crime to help you get in touch with some of the feelings that so often determine responses (for example, the murder of a child).

Close with a short time of reflection and prayer.

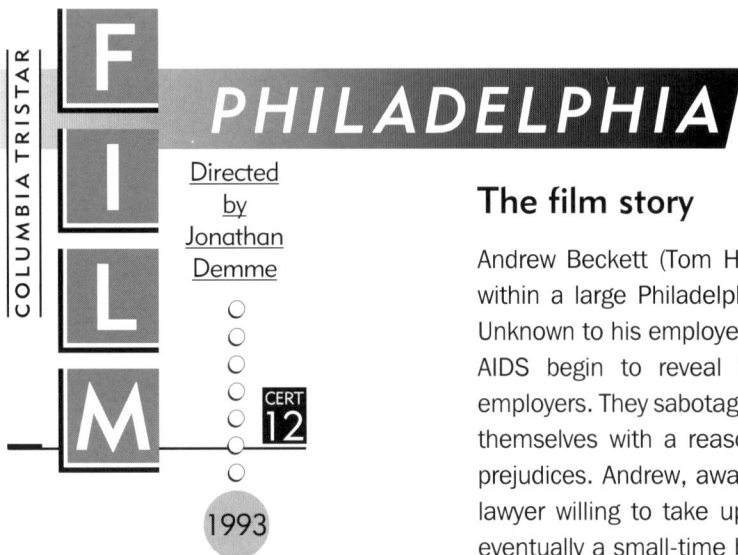

COLUMBIA TRISTAR

FILM

PHILADELPHIA

Directed
by
Jonathan
Demme

CERT **12**

1993

The film story

Andrew Beckett (Tom Hanks) is a young lawyer progressing rapidly up the ladder within a large Philadelphia law firm headed by Charles Wheeler (Jason Robards). Unknown to his employers, Andrew is gay and also HIV positive. As the symptoms of AIDS begin to reveal themselves, Andrew's illness becomes apparent to his employers. They sabotage an important case that he is involved with thereby providing themselves with a reason for dismissing him without revealing their deep-seated prejudices. Andrew, aware of what has happened, sets out to find a personal injury lawyer willing to take up his case against an immensely powerful legal firm. It is eventually a small-time black lawyer by the name of Joe Miller (Denzel Washington) who takes up Andrew's cause, but only after ridding himself of his own personal demons of prejudices against homosexuality and AIDS.

The film portrays an heroic struggle against intolerance and ignorance, set against Andrew's fight against the ravages of his illness. Though Andrew eventually loses his fight for life, there is a victory for justice.

Some key issues

Justice as a safeguard against prejudice – Andrew's victory in the courts shows justice at its best in recognising and ruling against the effects of discrimination.

The impartial nature of justice – true justice is not swayed by the influence of power but is concerned only with truth and fairness. The success of Joe Miller against the giant Philadelphia law firm in winning Andrew's case is a shining example.

The need to stand up against injustice – Andrew refuses to be intimidated by the power of his employers, and Joe takes the case against all the odds. Only in this way can injustice be exposed and challenged.

Clips

Show the section from the beginning of the film until the end of the conversation between Andy and Joe in the library.

Small group exercise:
In groups of three, each person imagine that you are either Andrew Beckett, Joe Miller, or Charles Wheeler (the head of the law firm who has sacked Andrew). In turn, talk with each other in character about your thoughts on Andrew's dismissal.

Group exercise:
Each small group to feed back, no longer in character, any significant points from the previous exercise.

Show the section from where Andy takes the stand in court to the point where he shows the court the lesions on his body.

Group discussion:
This harrowing film clip highlights the scale of the injustice that Andrew's law firm perpetrate against him because of their prejudice and ignorance. Identify any examples from life that you are aware of where prejudice and ignorance has been the root of injustice and talk with each other about these. How, in such instances, can justice prevail?

Our story

Small group discussion:
Talk with each other about any times in your own life when you or someone you know has been treated unjustly as a result of prejudice or ignorance. What effect did this have? Was any action taken to address the injustice? In hindsight, could anything different have been done in response?

Group activity:
What injustices are you currently aware of, a) in our own society and b) in the wider world? List these in two columns on a large sheet of paper.

Group discussion:
What do you see as the underlying causes for the injustices that you have listed? What would need to change to bring about justice? How might this happen?

God's story (same as for *A Time to Kill*)

Close with a short time of reflection and prayer.

SHADOWLANDS

Directed
by
Richard
Attenborough

CERT
U

1993

The film story

This is the true story of the love affair between C S "Jack" Lewis (Anthony Hopkins) and Joy Gresham (Debra Winger). Jack is a middle-aged Oxford lecturer and a prolific speaker and author in the field of Christian apologetics. Amongst his popular works are the Narnia stories, including *The Lion, The Witch and the Wardrobe*. Jack lives a sheltered academic's life, sharing a home with his brother Warnie (Edward Hardwicke). In contrast, Joy is an American who has a young son, Douglas (Joseph Mazzello), and whose marriage to an alcoholic husband is falling apart.

Joy exchanges correspondence with Jack, having "met" him through his writing. During a visit to England, she arranges to see him. Her refusal to be intimidated by Jack allows her to get beneath an exterior which, throughout his life, has caused him to function far more through intellect than emotion. When Joy next visits England, by now divorced, she brings Douglas with her. The couple grow close and Jack responds to Joy's request to marry her and enable her to share his British citizenship. At this point, Jack does not acknowledge any romantic attachment and after the civil wedding the couple continue to live separately.

Then tragedy strikes. Joy collapses suddenly and is diagnosed as having terminal cancer. This forces the love that Jack and Joy have for each other into the open and they are married by a priest at the hospital. For a while, Joy goes into remission and she, Jack and Douglas live together in Jack and Warney's home. As the film draws towards a poignant close and the death of Joy, there is a glimpse of C S Lewis, the great Christian apologist, experiencing from the inside the depth of grief and suffering which is the greatest test of Christian hope.

Some key issues
Hanging on in the darkness – Jack's life is devastated by Joy's illness and death.

Hope is far more than an idea – Jack has written much from a Christian perspective about finding hope in the middle of suffering. Personal tragedy tests the strength of his hope to the limit.

Hope and pain – Christian hope is no inoculation against the pain of life.

Clips

Show the section of film which lasts for approximately 15 minutes and encompasses Jack's speech about pain being "God's megaphone". This will help to illustrate the way in which Jack, at an intellectual level, was able to explain suffering.

Small group discussion:
Jack was able to offer some impressive arguments about the reason for suffering. What do you feel about his description of suffering as "God's megaphone"?

Show the last section from Jack and Joy's visit to the Herefordshire valley up to the end of the film.

Group discussion:

1.	Talk about the changes that took place in Jack. Pay particular attention to how you believe his faith was affected by Joy's illness and eventual death.

2.	In the attic, Douglas asked Jack if he believed in heaven. Jack's reply was yes, but even so he broke down under an almost unbearable grief. In what ways do you think Jack's hope of heaven helped him to come through his loss?

Our story

In pairs:
Share with each other an experience from your own lives where hope was pushed out by despair. Examples might be the illness or death of a loved one, or perhaps the loss of a job. What have you learned about your faith through that experience?

Small group exercise:
What are the things which cause people to lose hope? List as many items as you can on a large sheet of paper.

Group exercise:
Compare lists and identify common themes.

Group discussion:
Drawing from your own experiences, talk about the things that help you to cling on to hope in difficult times.

God's story

The world can be a frightening and bewildering place. In the midst of turmoil and suffering the heartfelt cry "Why, Lord?" has never been far from human lips. But God has never left his people bereft of hope. For the people of Old Testament times this hope was linked to the coming of the Messiah who would establish a peaceful and just rule (e.g. Isaiah 42.1–4; Isaiah 9.7; Jeremiah 23.5). Christians believe that the promise of the Messiah has been fulfilled in Jesus. Confirmation of this can be drawn from Jesus' quotation from the book of the prophet Isaiah (Luke 4.18–21).

There will, of course, continue to be sorrow and despair in the world as well as in our own lives in this "in-between" time. The Kingdom of God is present in the here and now but its fulfilment lies in the future. Our task is to embody and witness to the values of the Kingdom as we allow the presence of Christ to show through in our lives.

Although we are not immune to the suffering that all people face, as Christians we have an unquenchable hope that our eternal future is secure (John 3.16). Through the death and resurrection of Jesus Christ the final enemy of death has been defeated. We are also helped by the presence of the Holy Spirit to hang on to this hope even in the darkest of times. St Paul puts it very eloquently: "For I am certain that nothing can separate us from his love: neither death nor life, neither angels nor other heavenly rulers or powers, neither the present nor the future, neither the world above nor the world below – there is nothing in all creation that will ever be able to separate us from the love of God which is ours through Christ Jesus our Lord" (Romans 8.38, 39). For the Christian, hope is resting in the certainty that God's love will ultimately conquer all.

Small group activity:
Read Romans 8.18–39 which speaks of the future glory and God's love in Christ Jesus. Then work together to rewrite verses 38–39, drawing from some of the hardships that you saw in the film but also – more importantly – from your own life experience.

Group activity and discussion:
Invite each small group to share their "re-write" of Romans 8.38–39. Encourage people to talk about ways in which their Christian hope has pulled them through dark times.

In pairs:

Talk with each other about any particular passages from Scripture that have helped you cling on to hope during times of despair. (Do not worry if you cannot remember chapter and verse.)

Group activity:

Feedback the "hope-giving" passages from the pairs exercise. List these on a large sheet of paper, adding references where you can. (This could be produced later as a resource sheet).

Close with a short time of reflection and prayer.

FILM

RANK / CASTLE ROCK

THE SHAWSHANK REDEMPTION

Directed
by
Frank
Darabond

CERT
15

1994

The film story

Andy Dufresne (Tim Robbins), a city banker wrongly convicted of murdering his wife and her lover, arrives at Shawshank Prison in 1947 having received two consecutive life sentences. Andy is a quiet but intense person who is soon subjected to a severe beating and abuse from a particular group of inmates. To begin with, the only person who shows him friendship is Red (Morgan Freeman), the prison "fixer" from whom Andy obtains a small hammer which he uses to carve chess pieces from rocks. Slowly, Andy begins to win favours for his fellow inmates from the prison guards as he puts his accounting skills to use in completing the guards' tax returns. In one scene, a group on work duties enjoy some bottles of beer during a short respite from their labours.

Soon, Andy's skills earn him advantages too. He is put to work in the library, a recognition from Warden Norton (Bob Gunton) for his creative accountancy work which is securing Norton an illegal fortune. Unknown to the warden, Andy is also building a substantial bank account for himself in the name of an alias. Andy begins writing an endless flow of letters to charities to secure funds for a library extension, and eventually succeeds. There is also a time when Andy takes advantage of a guard's relaxed attitude and locks himself in the office from which he plays classical music over the prison's public address system. This earns him a stint in "the hole", but viewers are left feeling that Andy thought it worth the sacrifice to rekindle a spark of hope in the other prisoners' lives.

One morning, after twenty years in prison, the guards find that Andy is gone, having escaped through a tunnel hidden behind a poster and slowly hollowed out over two decades. Shortly after his escape, evidence of the Warden's corruption is sent by Andy to the authorities and Shawshank's crooked regime is overturned. The film ends with Red's eventual release from prison and his meeting up with Andy in Mexico on the shores of the Pacific, the place which had provided Andy with the hope to survive Shawshank Prison.

Some key issues

Hope despite the odds – Andy has been wrongly imprisoned and there is no way out, yet he refused to give in to despair.

The importance of something to hold on to – the little Mexican town on the shores of the big blue Pacific is Andy's motivation to survive Shawshank.

"Get busy living or get busy dying" – Andy chooses the former and survives the ordeal of his imprisonment.

Clips

Show the section of the film from where inattention gives Andy the opportunity to play a piece of music over the prison's public address system until the point when he is thrown into "the hole".

Group discussion:
Why do you think Andy made such a personal sacrifice in order for his fellow inmates to hear some music? Then try and imagine that you are an inmate at Shawshank Prison hearing music for the first time in years. How does it make you feel?

Show the section where, in the prison yard, Andy tells Red about his hope of living on the shores of the Pacific in Mexico.

Group discussion:
Throughout the film, Andy's dignity remained intact despite the brutality he suffered at the hands of both prison guards and some of the inmates. How important do you think Andy's hope was to his survival at Shawshank? Do you feel that Red, despite numerous rejections at the parole board, still had hope of one day being released?

Show the section from where Andy's escape is discovered through to the end of the film.

Group activity:
While Andy's hope enabled him to quietly plan his escape over twenty years, he was far from being self-centred. It was as if his hope spilled over into the way he treated his fellow inmates. List all the instances you can think of from the film where Andy's actions gave hope to others.

Our story

Small group discussion:
Think about any experiences of your own, or of any examples that you know of, where hanging on to hope has been significant in getting through a difficult time. Share these instances with each other. In what ways might your own experiences be of help to others whom you come across in despair?

Group discussion:
In the film, Andy's hope no doubt sounded more like a dream than anything of substance to Red. What difference, if any, is there between a hope and dream? Must every hope be achieved or is hope itself of intrinsic value?

Group activity:
On a large sheet of paper, invite each person to write in a sentence or two his or her hope for their lives. When everyone has done this, look for common threads and talk about how important these hopes are for surviving life's hard times.

God's story (same as for *Shadowlands*)

Close with a short time of reflection and prayer.

FORGIVENESS

DEAD MAN WALKING

Directed
by
Tim
Robbins

CERT
15

1995

The film story

Matthew Poncelet (Sean Penn) is on Death Row for his part in the murder of a teenage couple, Walter Delacroix (Peter Sarsgaard) and Hope Percy (Missy Yager), and has also been convicted of raping Hope before her murder. Sister Helen Prejean (Susan Sarandon), a Catholic nun working in a New Orleans slum, receives a letter from Matthew asking her to help him in his appeal for a pardon. At this stage he maintains his innocence.

Helen meets Matthew at the prison and, though disturbed, agrees to support him. As the film unfolds the relationship between Helen and Matthew intensifies. Helen searches for the humanity in Matthew and in Helen Matthew sees a face of love perhaps for the first time in his life. The parents of the murdered teenagers understandably find Sister Helen's involvement with Matthew difficult and feel their own pain is being overlooked. Forgiveness is far from their minds.

Eventually, all of Matthew's appeals are used up and the stark reality of his impending execution dawns upon him. For the first time, he acknowledges to Helen his guilt, and in the death chamber he asks the parents of the slain teenagers – there to witness his death – for their forgiveness. After Matthew's funeral there is a hint that the slain boy's father Earl (Raymond J. Barry) struggles to find forgiveness in his heart as he kneels side by side with Helen in a church.

Some key issues
The costly nature of forgiveness – how can the parents of Walter and Hope be expected to forgive their children's killer?

The relationship between forgiveness and remorse – almost until the very end, Matthew refuses to acknowledge his guilt.

Forgiveness and justice – Matthew's imprisonment is not in question; it is his execution that is challenged.

Clips

Show the section of film beginning with the last meeting of Matthew with his mother and brothers on the day of his execution and ending with the conversation between Matthew and Helen in which he admits his guilt. This is just before he is taken to the execution chamber.

Small group activity (two groups):
Group A:
Discuss the thoughts and feelings that you think were going on in Matthew's mind as he confesses to Helen his part in the murders. Then consider any ways in which your attitude towards Matthew is affected by his owning up to his crime. Be prepared to feed back the main points to the whole group.

Group B:
Discuss the thoughts and feelings that you think were going on in Helen's mind as she hears Matthew own up to his crime. What do you think Helen's motivation has been in working with Matthew? Be prepared to feed back the main points to the whole group.

Feedback session:
Each group to report back on its findings. Allow time for each group to ask and respond to questions and comments.

Show the final section, from Matthew being taken to the execution chamber until the end of the film.

In pairs:
Give each other the opportunity to share something of how this film clip has left you feeling. Then talk about your response to Matthew's appeal to the parents of his victims for forgiveness.

Group discussion:
What difference, if any, do you think that Matthew's confession and plea from the death chamber for forgiveness made to his victims' parents? Do you feel that forgiveness should be conditional upon remorse in the person seeking forgiveness?

Our story

Small group activity:
Take a moment to think about an example of a crime that you are aware of from the media which you would find particularly difficult to forgive. Talk about this with each other and list on a large sheet of paper what you see as the barriers to forgiveness. Compare your lists.

Group discussion:
Can you think of any times in your own life when you have found it difficult to forgive someone who had wronged you: how did it affect you? Can you think of any times when you have been forgiven for a wrong that you have committed and how did receiving that forgiveness make you feel?

God's story

Forgiveness lies at the heart of the Christian gospel. The starting point in forgiving others lies in recognising that God has already opened the way to our own forgiveness. All that we have done in life that has harmed our relationship with others and with God, individually and collectively, has been dealt with by Jesus Christ at the cross. He is the love and forgiveness of God embodied and our supreme example: "Anyone who is joined to Christ is a new being; the old has gone, the new has come. All this is done by God, who through Christ changed us from enemies into his friends and gave us the task of making others his friends also" (2 Corinthians 5.17, 18). A telling example of God's readiness to forgive is the story of the Lost Son (Luke 15.11–32). God's forgiveness is available to all who are sincerely sorry for the wrongs they have done – a gift that is there for the asking.

Forgiveness, of course, does not diminish the need for justice within human society. Our world is, after all, a broken world. But it does prevent the destructive effects of hatred and bitterness from being perpetuated and fed. And when forgiveness is truly sought from God we know that the slate is wiped clean because Christ has dealt with our wrongdoings in full.

In the prayer that Jesus taught us to pray we ask God to "Forgive us the wrongs we have done, as we forgive the wrongs that others have done to us" (Matthew 6.12). There is an important link here. God's love for us is unconditional, his offer of forgiveness always extended. However, forgiven people also need to be forgiving people and this is perhaps the hardest task of the Christian life. God wants us to allow our enjoyment of forgiveness to overflow into forgiveness towards others so that our enemies might become our friends. This will not always be easy, and might sometimes seem impossible, but it is the Bible's message and an ideal towards which we are called.

Group discussion:
Talk together about what it means to know that you are able to stand before God as forgiven people. How does it affect the way you live your life?

Group activity:
Read the story of the Lost Son (Luke 15:11–32). Try and imagine in turn, how the father, the lost son, and the elder son felt. This could be done by discussing each character in turn or by splitting into three-sub groups with members of each sub-group role-playing one of the characters.

Group discussion:
Which characters from the film ring bells with characters from the story of the Lost Son and why? When you think of your own life, are there moments when you identify yourself with one of the characters from the Lost Son story? Share these insights.

Group activity and discussion:
Read the Lord's Prayer (Matthew 6.9–13) and the Parable of the Unforgiving Servant (Matthew 18.21–35). Talk together about the implications of these readings for your own lives.

Close with a short time of reflection and prayer.

FILM

SECRETS AND LIES

Directed by Mike Leigh

CERT 15

1996

The film story

Hortense (Marianne Jean-Baptiste) is a young black woman working as an optometrist in London. Adopted as a child, she sets out to discover the identity of her true parents following the death of her mother. Her real mother, Cynthia (Brenda Blethyn), is a white, unmarried woman working in a dead-end job and living in a run-down terraced house with her daughter Roxanne (Claire Rushbrook). Roxanne is approaching her twenty-first birthday and works as a road sweeper. Cynthia's brother, Maurice (Timothy Spall), has a successful photography business and is married to Monica (Phyllis Logan), who snobbishly looks down on Cynthia. As a result, Maurice and Cynthia seldom meet and when they do, the painfulness of the relationship is apparent. But with Roxanne's birthday approaching, Maurice offers to hold a party for Roxanne at his home.

In the meantime, Hortense has managed to track down Cynthia's whereabouts and after some traumatic telephone conversations meets with Cynthia at a cafeteria in Holborn. Hortense discovers that she was conceived when her mother was a teenager and given up for adoption without Cynthia ever seeing her. Cynthia believed that the baby was premature and the result of a later relationship. She has never realised therefore that the child she gave away was black.

Cynthia and Hortense become friends and when the day of Roxanne's birthday party comes around, Cynthia takes her along. At the party, Cynthia reveals that Hortense is her daughter. The initial effect is devastating: Roxanne storms out; Monica reveals that she cannot have children; and Maurice owns up to the stress within his marriage. However, with the uncovering of all these secrets and lies the film shows how acceptance and forgiveness brings the family back together.

Some key issues

The damaging effect of secrets and lies – Roxanne, at first, is devastated to discover that she has a sister that her mother has never spoken of; Maurice and Monica have the trappings of a successful marriage but underneath are struggling badly.

The need for truth and openness – only when the facts are brought to light does forgiveness and healing become possible.

The costly nature of truth – carefully weighs up the implications of trying to find her natural mother, aware of the painful emotions and past hurts that will need to be faced.

Clips

Show the section of the film that begins with Hortense's first telephone call to Cynthia, up to and including the conversation between them in the cafeteria at Holborn.

Group discussion:
In this meeting with Hortense, Cynthia's past catches up with her. Talk about what you think must have been going on for Cynthia as she met her daughter for the first time. Repeat the exercise, this time trying to see things from Hortense's point of view.

Show the section from the arrival of Cynthia at Maurice's for Roxanne's party through to the end of the film.

Group discussion:
Talk about the reasons for the secrets and lies to have been maintained for so long. Why do you think Cynthia had never told Roxanne about her sister? Why did Maurice and Monica feel the need to keep secret Monica's inability to have children?

Our story

Small group discussion:
Families are complicated and, for all sorts of reasons, it is often within families that we are hurt most. Share with each other, if you feel able, some examples from your own life.

Group discussion:
Thinking of the personal experiences just shared in the small groups, talk about the things that get in the way of forgiveness. These could be listed on a large sheet of paper and used as a focus for prayer at the end of the session.

Group discussion:
Though forgiveness is sometimes difficult to give, it is a wonderful gift to receive. Take a moment to recall a time in your life when you experienced forgiveness from another human being. Share something of what that forgiveness felt like with each other.

God's story (same as for *Dead Man Walking*)

Close with a short time of reflection and prayer.

References

1. **A Bigger Picture: The report of the Film Policy Review Group**, p,12.

2. Eddie (editor), **The BFI Film and Television Handbook 1998**, p.31.

3. ibid, p.32.

4. ibid, p.33.

5. ibid, p.43.

6. ibid, p.50.

7. ibid, p.46.

8. Clive Marsh and Ortiz, **Explorations in Theology and Film**, p.19.

9. Alan Macdonald, **Films in Close-up,** p.15.

Bibliography

A Bigger Picture: The report of the Film Policy Review Group, The Department of Culture, Media and Sport, 1998.

Bone, I & Johnson, R, **Understanding the Film: An Introduction to Film Appreciation (5th edition),** 1996.

Dyja, E, (ed.), **The BFI Film and Television Handbook 1998**, The British Film Institute, 1997.

Macdonald, A, **Films in Close-up**, Frameworks, 1991.

Marsh, C & Ortiz, G, **Explorations in Theology and Film**, Blackwell, 1997.

Walker, J, **Halliwell's Film and Video Guide**, HarperCollins, 1996.

BRITISH AND FOREIGN BIBLE SOCIETY
Stonehill Green, Westlea, Swindon, SN5 7DG, England
© 1998 Bible Society

Unless otherwise stated, quotations from the Bible are from the Good News Bible, published by the Bible Societies/HarperCollins Publishers Ltd UK © American Bible Society, New York 1966, 1971, 1976 and 1992.

A catalogue record for this book is available from the British Library ISBN 0564 041262.

Printed in Great Britain by Swindon Press
Cover illustration by Jeff Roberts
Design, typography and typesetting by British and Foreign Bible Society Graphic Services

Bible Societies exist to provide resources for Bible distribution and use. The British and Foreign Bible Society (BFBS) is a member of the United Bible Societies, an international partnership working in over 180 countries. Their common aim is to reach all people with the Bible, or some part of it, in a language they can understand and at price they can afford. Parts of the Bible have now been translated into over 2,000 languages. Bible Societies aim to help every church at every point where it uses the Bible. You are invited to share in this work by your prayers and gifts. The Bible Society in your country will be very happy to provide details of its activity.